Boomax Saves the Day

Carmel Reilly
Ned Culic

Rigby

www.Rigby.com
1-800-531-5015

Rigby Focus Forward

This Edition © 2009 Rigby, a Harcourt Education Imprint

Published in 2007 by Nelson Australia Pty Ltd ACN: 058 280 149
A Cengage Learning company

1 2 3 4 5 6 7 8 374 14 13 12 11 10 09 08 07
Printed and bound in China

Ben Fox Saves the Day
ISBN-13   978-1-4190-3665-1
ISBN-10   1-4190-3665-3

Ben Fox Saves the Day

Carmel Reilly
Ned Culic

Contents

Chapter 1

Stop That Boy!

One day, Ben Fox went to the shop
for his mom.

He was outside the shop
getting oranges out of a box
when the woman
from the shop shouted,
"Stop him! Stop him!"

Ben looked up at the woman.

"See that boy running away?"
she shouted.
"He has my bag!"

Ben looked down the street.

"I can see a boy.
He has a blue shirt and black shorts on,
and he has a red bag," Ben said.

"Yes, that is him," said the woman.
"And that is my bag!"

"Stay here," said Ben to the woman.
"I will get your bag back for you."

Chapter 2

In the Park

As Ben ran up the street,
he looked down.

"Oh, no!" he said,
"I still have my bag of oranges."

But he did not have time to stop.

The boy ran across the street
and into the park.

Ben looked up and down the street.
He did not see any cars.

Ben ran across the street after the boy.
Then he went into the park, too.

At the park,
Ben looked around.

Children played
on the swings.

Ben looked past
the children and
into some trees.

"I can see you now!" he shouted.

The boy ran out of the trees.

"You can't get me!" he said.

"Yes, I can!" said Ben.

The boy went on running,
and Ben ran after him.

The boy ran past the children.
Ben ran past the children, too.

"Stop!" Ben shouted.

But the boy did not stop.

Ben looked down at his bag of oranges.
He had an idea.

Chapter 3

The Bag of Oranges

Ben rolled the oranges over the grass.

The boy did not see the oranges coming. The oranges rolled under his feet …

The boy fell over,
and the woman's bag went flying
into a tree.

"I will take *that* back now," said Ben
as he went over to get it.

"Here is your bag," said Ben.

"Oh, thank you," said the woman.

"I still have to buy some oranges
for my mom," said Ben.

"Here!" said the woman.
"Have this box of oranges
as a thank you for all your help."